In the Name of Allah, the Most Beneficent, Most Merciful...

And when it is said to them. "Come to what Allah has revealed and to the Messenger (Muhammad ﷺ for the verdict of that which you have made unlawful)" they say: "Enough for us is that which we found our fathers following." Even though their fathers had no knowledge whatsoever nor guidance.

(Qur'an 5: 104)

Browsing through a book do's not indicate reading it .

THE
MESSAGE
OF
ISLAM

BY:

Abdul Rahman -A- AL-Sheha

Translated by:

Ghalib Ahmad Masri

Riyadh, Kingdom of Saudi Arabia
1422 H. = 2001 G.

4th Eddition

© Abdur Rahman Al-Sheha, 2000

King Fahd National Library Cataloging-in-Publication Data
Al- Sheha, Abdur Rahman
The message of Islam - Riyadh
160 p 14.5 X 21 cm.
ISBN: 9960-36-874-2
1- Islam - General principles   I- Title
210 dc   0488/21

Legal Deposit no. 0488/21
ISBN : 9960-36-874-2
ISSN : 1319-2868

Dear Reader,

Islam is a complete and integral Divine religion and way of life. It has a complete code of ethics for a happy life and peaceful and tranquil life after death.

Islam is pure from all imperfections, defects and blemishing effects. It is a perfect way of life.

Any deviant or abnormal behavior observed on a Muslim should have no bearing on Islam, non-what-so-ever. The reason for such a deviation or bad behavior is due to ill knowledge of the faith itself, or due a weak faith that led to such deviant acts.

Islam, by no mean, should be assessed or evaluated based on the individuals' behavior and attitudes.

Say, "O People of the Book, come to a word that is equitable between us and you - that we will not worship except Allah and not associate anything with Him and not take one another as lords instead of Allah,[1] But if they turn away, then say, "Bear witness that we are Muslims [submitting to Him]."

(Qur'an 3: 64)

---

(1) By obeying another in disobedience to Allah.

Table of Contents

محتويات الكتاب

٧. حقوق الجيران .

٨. حقوق الأصحاب .

٩. حقوق الضيوف .

١٠. حقوق العمال والأجراء .

١١. حقوق أصحاب العمل .

١٢. حقوق عامة .

- المأمورات والمنهيات في الإسلام .
- الجانب الأخلاقي في الإسلام .
- **الآداب الإسلامية :-**

١. آداب الأكل .

٢. آداب الاستئذان .

٣. آداب السلام .

٤. آداب الجلوس .

٥. آداب المجلس .

٦. آداب المحادثة .

٧. آداب المزاح .

٨. آداب العزاء .

٩. آداب النوم .

١٠. آداب المعاشرة الزوجية .

١١. آداب السفر .

١٢. آداب البيع والشراء .

✿   ✿   ✿

INTRODUCTION

All praise is due to Allah. May Allah's peace and blessings be upon His messenger Muhammad, his companions, his family and his followers until the day resurrection.

I am very happy to introduce this book (the Message of Islam) to all readers (Muslims and non-Muslims) for two reasons: the first is that I know brother Abd al-Raman al-Sheha for about a year now. I have dealt with him and found him to be one of the finest people I have met. By the grace of Allah, he has a good character and he is dedicated to the cause of serving Allah to the best. The second is that I find this book to be interesting and beneficial. The reader, whether being a Muslim or not, will find a presentation that is logical, orderly, and supported with evidence. I also find this book to be easy to read while containing all the necessary information about Islam.

The subject of this book is important not only because we need to refine our understanding of Islam, but also because many people don't have a comprehensive and yet detailed concept of Allah's way of life. Many followers of Islam limit the role of religion into mere acts of worship confined to the mosque or in times of hardships and difficulties. This is an incomplete and distorted understanding of Islam. Allah is perfect and His religion (or way of life) is complete and comprehensive. It is the fault of some followers of Islam who project this great and beautiful religion in a bad image.

As a reader, you need to read the entire book, so that you will know to what extent religion covers every aspect of one's daily life. I am sure that at the end, by Allah's grace, you will pray for the author and you will be inwardly and outwardly rewarded.

I pray that Allah would reward my brother Abd al- Rahman Al-Sheha for writing this book and for all his effort in the cause of serving Islam, Muslims and humanity. All praise is due to Allah the Almighty.

Dr. Ahmad Ibn Saifuddin
Associate Professor
Imam Muhammad bin Sa'ud
Islamic University
Riyadh, Saudi Arabia

Preface

**In the Name of Allah, the Most Beneficent, Most Merciful...
Praise be to Allah, Peace and blessings of Allah be upon His
Messenger, Muhammad, and all his family and companions.**

Allah, the Exalted, says, (the meaning of which is translated as):

> *"Say: 'O People of the Scripture! Come to a word that is
> just between us and you: that we shall worship none but
> Allah, and that we shall ascribe no partner unto Him, and
> that none of us shall take others for Lords besides Allah.'
> Then, if they turn away, say: 'Bear witness that we are
> Muslims.'" (The Qur'aan, Chapter Ali 'Imran, 3:64).*

Islam is the religion of pure human nature and clarity. It urges and
calls its followers to ask about all things that are incomprehensible to
them or the questions that occur to them. They are recommended to
consult competent, knowledgeable authorities. In Islam there are no
obscure or mysterious things that we have only to believe without
being allowed to ask about them. Allah, Glory to Him says, (the
meaning of which is translated as):

> *"...So ask the followers of the scriptures if you know not."
> (The Qur'aan, Chapter An-Nahl, 16:43).*

As human beings, we have many questions in our mind that require
answers, which should be logical, convincing and unambiguous
ones... It is the Noble Qur'aan which provides such answers in such
fluent, convincing, and incomparable style. Let us observe these basic
queries:

- If man inquires about his origin, he will find the answer in
Almighty Allah's saying, (the meaning of which is translated
as):

> *"And indeed We created man (Adam) out of an extract of
> clay. Thereafter We placed him as (a drop of) sperm in a
> place of rest firmly fixed. Then We made the sperm into a
> clot of congealed blood; then of that clot We made a (fetus)
> lump; then We made out of that lump bones and clothed the
> bones with flesh; then We developed out of it another
> creature. So blessed be Allah, the Best of Creators."(The
> Qur'aan, Chapter Al-Mu'minun, 23:12-14)*

2

- If he inquires about his status in this Universe and his rank among other creatures, he will find the answer in the following verse, (the meaning of which is translated as):

"And indeed We have honored the children of Adam and We have carried them on land and sea and have provided them with good and pure things and have preferred them above many of those whom We have created with a marked preference." (The Qur'aan, Chapter Al-Isra', 17:70).

- If he also inquires about the cause of his creation, he will find the answer in the following verses, (the meaning of which is translated as):

"And I (Allah) have only created the jinn and mankind that they may worship Me (alone). No sustenance do I require of them nor do I require that they should feed Me. For Allah is He who gives (all) sustenance, Lord of Power, the Most Strong." (The Qur'aan Chapter Adh-Dhariyat, 51:56-58)

"Did you then think that We had created you in jest and that you would not be brought back to us (for account)? So Exalted is Allah, the True King:There is no god but He, the Lord of the Throne of Honor!" (The Qur'aan Chapter Al-Mu'minun, 23:115-116).

- If man then asks about this Creator Who is the only One worthy of worship, he will find the answer in the following words, (the meaning of which is translated as):

"He is Allah beside Whom there is no other god, Who knows the unseen and the seen, He is the All-Beneficent, All-Merciful. He is Allah, beside Whom there is no other god; - the Sovereign, the Holy One, the Source of Peace (and Perfection), the Guardian of Faith, the Watcher over His creatures, the Exalted in Might, the Irresistible, the Supreme. Glory to Allah! (High is He) above all that they associate as partners with Him. He is Allah, the Creator, the Maker (of all things), the Giver of forms. To Him belong the Most Beautiful Names. Whatever is in the heavens and the earth, glorify Him:And He is the All-Mighty, the All-Wise." (The Qur'aan, Chapter Al-Hashr, 59:22-24)

THE MESSAGE OF ISLAM

• If he asks about the attitude he should assume with the things Allah has created for him in this universe, he will find the answer in the following verse, (the meaning of which is translated as):

"O you who believe! Eat of the lawful things that We have provided for you, and be grateful to Allah, if it is Him you worship." (The Qur'aan, Chapter Al-Baqarah, 2:172).

• If he inquires about the true religion that he should embrace and the path which leads to happiness in this life and in the hereafter, he will surely find the response in the Qur'aanic verse, (the meaning of which is translated as):

"And whoever seeks a religion other than Islam, it will never be accepted of him; and in the Hereafter he will be one of the losers." (The Qur'aan Chapter Ali 'Imran, 3:85)

• If he inquires, too, about the path that leads to peace of mind/heart and mental stability, he will find the answer in the following words, (the meaning of which is translated as):

"Those who have believed and whose hearts find rest in the remembrance of Allah: verily, in the remembrance of Allah do hearts find rest." (The Qur'aan, Chapter Ar-Ra'd, 13:28)

• If he asks about the state (position) of those who lack belief in Allah, Glory to Him, and in His revelations, he will get the answer in the following, (the meaning of which is translated as):

"But whosoever turns away from My Reminder (i.e.:My Message), verily for him is a life of hardship and We shall raise him up blind on the Day of Resurrection." (The Qur'aan Chapter Taha, 20:124).

• If he asks about his destiny in this life, he will find the answer in these words, (the meaning of which is translated as):

"Every soul shall taste of death. And only on the Day of Resurrection shall you be paid your wages in full. Whosoever is removed from the Fire and admitted to Paradise, he is indeed successful. The life of this world is but

a comfort of illusion." (The Qur'aan, Chapter Ali 'Imran, 3:185).

• If he inquires about the possibility of re-creating him, he will find a satisfactory answer in Allah's words, (the meaning of which is translated as):

"And if he has coined (compared) for Us a similitude, and has forgotten the fact of his creation, saying:Who will revive these bones when they have rotted away? Say: He will revive them Who produced them the first time, for He is All-Knower of every creation." (The Qur'aan Chapter Yasin, 36:78-79).

And in the following words, (the meaning of which is translated as):

"O mankind! If you are in doubt concerning the Resurrection, then Lo! We have created you from dust, then from a drop of sperm, then from a clot, then from a little lump of flesh shapely and shapeless, that We may make (it) clear for you. And We cause what We will to remain in the wombs for an appointed time and afterward We bring you forth as infants..." (The Qur'aan, Chapter Al-Hajj, 22:5)

If he asks what will happen after death, the answer will delineate that the matter is one of eternal life after death and resurrection: That is, the destination will be either eternity in Paradise or in Hell, and there is no third destination, (the meaning of which is translated as):

"Lo! Those who disbelieve among the people of the scripture and the idolaters, will abide in the Fire of Hell. They are the worst of created beings. And Lo! Those who believe and do good works are the best of created beings. Their reward is with their Lord:Gardens of Eden underneath which rivers flow, wherein they dwell forever. Allah has pleasure in them and they have pleasure in Him. This is (in store) for him who fears his Lord." (The Qur'aan, Chapter Al-Baiyina, 98:6-8).

Dear reader:

I shall reaffirm that Islam offers optimum solutions to all current problems of the world and that implementation of the Islamic way of life, will, by all means, resolve such problems. The World has tried all doctrines that proved with the passage of time, to be incapable of solving its problems. So why does the World not accept the Islamic way of life and implement it for the well-being of the humanity.

F. Filweas,[1] as well as some western writers and philosophers, claiming that;

"Recent newspapers have published articles insinuating that Philosophy and Western writings claim that contemporary religions have become outdated and should be given up. This reveals the pessimism which most Western writers suffer from due to the complexities and obscurities they find in Christianity. Yet they have committed a grave mistake because Islam is the religion which provides the uniquely perfect response that never stops answering – and in the face of every change – it will still be ready to respond."

Dear reader;

Truthfully speaking, I regret to say that some Muslims nowadays are quite far from actual implementation of Islam's principles and instructions. Unfortunately, they are Muslims only by name and not in the exact meaning of the word. A true Muslim takes the Glorious Qur'aan and the Pure Prophetic Sunnah, the main sources of Islam, as his way of life and code of conduct to which he adheres in all his/her private and public dealings and transactions. A real Muslim is not one who takes those aspects of Islam that suit his own interests, even at the expense of others' interests, while leaving what is in conflict with his own interests even though it is in is in the best interest of others.

It is absolutely unfair to associate Islam with certain countries or persons. It is wrong and improper to say that practices of the majority of Muslims nowadays in their real actual everyday life in full agreement with Islam's sublime teachings and objectives. The greatest majority of Muslims are quite far from practicing Islam. Islam is not, as some may think, mere religious rites that are practiced at set times only; rather, it comprises belief, law, devotions, transactions and dealings:It is a religion as well as a governmental system, in the full

---

[1] A British naval officer who participated in both World Wars. He was raised as a Christian having a strong belief in the Messiah. Yet he embraced Islam in 1924 after he studied the Noble Qur'aan and a number of books on Islam. See "What they say about Islam" by Amad Ad-Din Khalil

meaning of the word. It has been said, "What a great religion, if only there had been men who put its principles and teachings into action, complied with its commandments and avoided its prohibitions."

In his book, "Arab Civilization", Mr. J. S. Restler mentioned three different meanings for the term Islam: *"The first as religion, the second as state and government, and the third as culture - in short: it is a unique civilization."*

ISLAM is with its belief, devotions, dealings and law (i.e. Sharia), since it was revealed unto Prophet Muhammad, peace be upon him, and is still the same as it was. No change or alteration has occurred to it. It is the people called Muslims who have undergone change and transformation. If one who calls himself a Muslim commits a mistake or something unlawful, this does not mean that Islam enjoins or accepts such behavior. If someone is given, for example, a dismantled vehicle and provided with a comprehensive accurate erection plan (Installation manual) from the manufacturer, but he assembles it incorrectly, can we say that the plan (manual) is incorrect? Rather it should be stated that this person has failed to follow the exact steps in an appropriate manner or to put the procedure fully into effect.

I would kindly invite (request) every reader of this work to have a detached mind, not influenced by religious sentiments or mental biases, with the aim of attaining the truth, not searching for faults and blunders for the sake of slander. The reader is also invited to read seeking to understand through his mind, not through his emotional views, lest he be of those censured by Allah as stated in the Glorious Qur'aan, (the meaning of which is translated as):

"And when it is said unto them:Follow that which Allah has revealed, they Say: We follow that wherein we found our fathers, What! Even though their fathers were wholly unintelligent and had no guidance?" (The Qur'aan, Chapter Al-Baqarah, 2:170).

That is because a reasonably logical-minded man will not accept a thing unless he has studied it thoroughly and grown familiar with it. When he acquires such familiarity and becomes fully satisfied about its validity, he should not keep it to himself. Rather, he should disseminate his knowledge among people, thereby teaching the ignorant and correcting those who are mistaken.

I shall admit here that I have not covered or researched the subject thoroughly. That is because when you speak about Islam you speak, in fact, about a comprehensive, all-embracing law which regulates all affairs pertaining to both worldly life and the hereafter. This will in fact, require a book, not a booklet, for explanation. However, I have only made hints on certain principles and basic morals of Islam that pave the way for those who desire to know more about the truth of Islam, supported by verses from the Noble Qur'aan which is the code of conduct for Muslims, and the sayings of Prophet Muhammad, peace be upon him.

One may say : the laws and regulations of contemporary societies have some similarities to those of Islam. In answer we may ask:Which is earlier:Has Islam preceded contemporary laws? The Islamic Sharia (Law) is over fourteen centuries older than these regulations and laws. Whatever is similar to Islamic laws and regulations may probably be derived from them. We know that there were studies concerned with Islam by non-Muslims, particularly orientalists, with different intentions and objectives, since the beginning of its appearance.

Abdur-Rahman A. Al-Sheha
WWW.ISLAMLAND.ORG-WWW.COCG.ORG
E-mail ALSHEHA@COCG.ORG
P.O. Box 59565,
Riyadh 11535,
Saudi Arabia

The Issue of Monotheism in Islam

Islam, like other revealed religions, advocates several precepts and beliefs that Allah has required its followers to believe in and propagate without coercion, in keeping with Allah's commandment, (the meaning of which is translated as):

"There is no compulsion in religion..." (The Qur'aan, Chapter Al-Baqarah, 2:256)

One of Islam's fundamentals is the belief in the Oneness of Allah, glory to Him, and directing worship to Him alone. This is the thing for which Allah has created mankind and sent messengers as He said, (the meaning of which is translated as):

"Say: 'He is Allah, the One! Allah, the eternally besought of all! He begets not, nor was begotten. And there is none comparable unto Him.'" (The Qur'aan, Chapter Al-Ikhlas, 112:1-4)

This involves refraining from ascribing partners to Allah, as obvious from Allah's words, (the meaning of which is translated as):

"Indeed Allah pardons not that partners should be ascribed unto Him. He pardons all save that to whom He wills..." (The Qur'aan, Chapter An-Nisa'a, 4:116)

Islam ascribes the attributes of perfection to Him and glorifies and exalts Him above His creation as in the following verse, (the meaning of which is translated as):

"...There is nothing like Him, and He is the All-Hearer, the All-seer." (The Qur'aan, Chapter Ash-Shura, 42:11).

It has produced proofs of Allah's oneness in matters of creation, ruling out any possibility of having any partners Allah said, (the meaning of which is translated as):

"Had there been therein (in the heavens and the earth) gods besides Allah, then verily both would have been ruined..." (The Qur'aan, Chapter Al-Anbiya', 21:22).

"...or each god would have assuredly taken away what he had created, and some of them would assuredly have

overcome others...." (The Qur'aan, Chapter Al-Mu'minun 23:91).

It has also called upon man to reflect on his self, the thing closest to him, so that through it he should see, the greatness and majesty of the Creator. Allah said, (the meaning of which is translated as):

"And (also) in yourselves, can you then not see? (The Qur'aan, Chapter Az-Zariyat, 51:21).

It is a call to meditation and reasoning which leads common sense and pure nature to believe in the greatness of Allah.

The human soul is given, since its creation, to recognize the existence of it's Creator who has also created this Universe, which demonstrates the greatness of its Creator. That is what scientists call 'religious inborn instinct or nature; Allah –glorious is He – says, (the meaning of which is translated as):

"So set your face(i.e;self) toward the religion as a man by nature upright – the nature (framed) of Allah, in which He has created man..." (The Qur'aan, Chapter Ar-Rum, 30:30)

This nature is inherent in all people without exception. However, some people deny it out of abstinence and pride, while others acknowledge and believe in it. It's being inherent in everyone is evidenced by the fact that it comes out when it is aroused. When a person falls ill, for instance, or he is struck by an evil or surprised by something unpleasant, you find that he unconsciously cries. O God! Or he just raises his eyes to heaven, recognizing the existence of a great mighty power that is able to save him from his dilemma. This is only depicted in Allah's words, (the meaning of which is translated as):

"And if misfortune touches a man, he cries unto Us (while reclining) on his side or sitting or standing, but when We have relieved him of the misfortune he goes his way as though he had not cried unto Us because of a misfortune that afflicted him." (The Qur'aan, Chapter Yunus, 10:12).

Islam replied to those who were tempted into denying the Almighty Creator by a negative question, Allah said the, meaning of which is translated as:

"Or were they created out of nothing? Or were they (themselves) the Creators? Or did they create the heavens and the earth? Nay, but they are sure of nothing!" (The Qur'aan, Chapter Fatir, 52:35-36).

If it is impossible for man to come into being by accident, i.e.: without for man to create or bring himself into existence. Common sense and upright nature would admit that every being requires a creator and every effect involves a cause, thus remains the third possibility, i.e. the existence of a Creator. One nomad (bedouin), when asked how he knew about the existence of Allah, said, (the meaning of which is translated as):

"Droppings suggest the existence of 'camel, and footprints are a sign of walking. How about a sky holding mansions of the stars and an earth with tracks and passes; Don't they indicate the existence of the Most Kind, All-Aware God?

Fundamentals of Islam

Among the most important fundamentals of Islam are: *prohibition of aggression against life, honor, wealth, mind, offspring, or against the weak and the disabled.*

About the immunity and inviolability of life, the Qur'aan says, (the meaning of which is translated as):

"And slay not the life which Allah has forbidden save with right..." (The Qur'aan, Chapter Al-Isra', 17:33).

About the sanctity of honor Allah said, (the meaning of which is translated as):

"O you who believe! Let not a folk deride a folk who may be better than they (are), nor let women (deride) women who may be better than they are..." (The Qur'aan, Chapter Al-Hujurat, 49:11).

"Who so commits a delinquency or crime, then casts (the blame) thereof upon someone innocent, has burdened himself with falsehood and a flagrant crime." (The Qur'aan, Chapter An-Nisa'a, 4:112)

On the prohibition of trespassing against crops and offspring (of animals or people) Allah said, (the meaning of which is translated as):

"And when he turns away (from you), his effort in the land is to make mischief therein and to destroy the crops and offspring; and Allah does not love mischief."(The Qur'aan, Chapter Al-Baqarah, 2:205)

When speaking about the rights of the weak, the Qur'aan states the rights of parents, (the meaning of which is translated as):

"And your Lord has decreed that you worship none save (except) Him, and (that you show) kindness to parents. If one of them or both of them attain old age with you, say not "Fie" to them nor repulse them, but speak to them a graceful word." (The Qur'aan, Chapter Al-Isra', 17:23)

And also the rights of orphans, (the meaning of which is translated as):

"Therefore, the orphan oppress not." *(The Qur'aan, Chapter Ad-Duha, 93:9)*

"Come not near the wealth of the orphan save with that which is better (to improve it)." (The Qur'aan, Chapter Al-Isra', 17:34)

And the rights of children, (the meaning of which is translated as):

"...And then you slay not your children because of poverty – We provide for you and for them." (The Qur'aan, Chapter Al-An'am, 6:151)

On the rights of the sick, the Messenger of Allah, Muhammad (pbuh)[2] says:

"Give food (to the poor), visit the sick, and help to release prisoners from captivity." (Narrated by Imam Bukhari).

On the rights of the elderly, the Prophet (pbuh) says:

"Glorification of Allah involves honoring Muslims who grow old."

He (pbuh) also says, (the meaning of which is translated as):

"He is not one of us who does not respect our old people and have no mercy with our little children."

This is all summed up in the following Hadith (Prophets' famous speech in the farewell speech):

"Your blood, property and honor are as sacred to you, as sacred as this day of yours, in this city of yours, and in this month of yours." (Narrated by Imam Bukhari)

All people are equal in such matters. This does not mean that other good morals are minor things in Islamic Law. In fact, they are duties that Muslims must stick to.

---

[2] This symbol is short of " May the peace and blessings of Allah be upon him"

Features of Islam that Distinguish it from other Religions

1. Islamic texts have explicitly stated that religion, to Allah, is one and the same, that the prophets sent by Allah to mankind complement each other. These prophets began with Adam, peace be upon him, up to Muhammad (pbuh) and the messages of those prophets and messengers are in agreement about calling to the following:

- Belief in the Oneness of Allah, glorious is He, with no associates, equals or likes.
- Belief in Allah, His angels, books, messengers, and the Hereafter.
- Good manners and refinement of the human self by guiding it to the way of reform and happiness in this life and the Hereafter.
- Direct worship of Almighty Allah without the intervention of any intermediaries in worship.
- The establishment of peace and love in human societies. Allah, glory to Him, says, (the meaning of which is translated as):

"He has ordained for you the same religion that He commended unto Noah, and that which We have revealed to you (O Muhammad), and that which We commended unto Abraham and Moses and Jesus saying:Establish the religion, and be not divided therein. Dreadful for the idolaters is that unto which you call them." (The Qur'aan, Chapter Ash-Shura, 42:13)

2. The Islamic Religion is the final and concluding Shari'ah or way of life: there is no religion to follow. Its primal constitution, which is the Glorious Qur'aan, is permanent and preserved and will remain up to the end of this world and all living things. This is indicated in the Qur'aan, (the meaning of which is translated as):

"Lo! We, even We, have revealed the Reminder (Qur'aan) and Lo! We verily are its Guardian". (The Qur'aan, Chapter An-Nahl, 15:9).

- Allah's Messenger (pbuh) is the last of messengers. There is no messenger or prophet after him. Prophet Muhammad, (pbuh) said,

"My similitude in comparison with the other prophets before me, is that of a man who has built a house nicely and beautifully, except for a space for one brick in a corner". The people go about it and wonder at its beauty, they Say: "Would that this brick be put in its place!' So I am that brick, and I am the last of the prophets." *(Bukhari)*

Issa (Jesus), however will come down in the last days of this world to fill the world with justice as it was filled with oppression and injustice. He will not be sent with a new religion as indicated by the last Prophet, Muhammed (pbuh) who said:

"The son of Mariam (i.e.:Jesus son of Mary) will soon descend among you as a Just Rule. He will break the cross, kill the pigs, put an end to jizya[3], and wealth will be in such abundance that no one will accept it." *(Imam Ahmad & Bukhari).*

To accept this universality, Muslims have been ordered to convey the Message of Islam and present it to mankind as stated in the Qur'aan, (the meaning of which is translated as):

"Thus We have appointed you a middle nation, that you may be witnesses over mankind, and that the Messenger may be a witness over you..." *(The Qur'aan, Chapter Al-Baqarah, 2:143)*

3. Islam completed and perfected the former religious codes which were spiritual in their roots. They addressed the human self and called to its purification, but did not take care or regulate worldly and living affairs, in contrast with Islam, which completed and regulated all aspects of life. It has covered all religious and worldly affairs, as will be made clear later. Allah has stated, (the meaning of which is translated as):

---

[3] A tax taken from rich non-Muslims for defending them if they choose do not participate in defense of the nation.

"...This day have I perfected your religion for you and completed My favor for you, and have chosen for you Islam as your religion..." (The Qur'aan, Chapter Al-Mai'dah, 5:3)

4. Allah, glory to Him, does not accept that devotion should be directed to other than Him or that anyone or anything should be worshipped as an intermediary between people and their Lord. He said, (the meaning of which is translated as):

"And whoever seeks a religion other than Islam, it will never be accepted from him, and in the Hereafter he will be among the losers." (The Qur'aan, Chapter Ali 'Imran, 3:85)

5. Islam is a universal message addressed to the whole of humanity without exception, in every place and in every time. This message is addressed to humans and jinns,(an unseen creature like mankind created by Allah from fire) Arabs and non-Arabs, blacks and whites, male and female, poor and rich. Allah, says, (the meaning of which is translated as):

"And We have not sent You (O Muhammad) except as a bearer of good news and a Warner to all mankind..." (The Qur'aan, Chapter Saba, 34:28)

It is a universal religion:not revealed or sent exclusively to one race, class or nation. It unites all people, not on the basis of color, language, region, or lineage, but on basis of a specific creed that combines and unifies them all. Everyone who believes in Allah as his Lord, in Islam as his religion, and in Muhammad (pbuh) as his Messenger, has come under the banner of Islam. Allah, glory to Him, says, (the meaning of which is translated as):

"Say (O Muhammad):O mankind! Lo! I am the Messenger of Allah to you all..." (The Qur'aan, Chapter Al-A'raf, 7:158)

Allah's Messenger, (pbuh) said,

"I have been granted five (things) which were not granted to anyone before me. I have been supported by a form of fright that spans the distance of one month's travel. The earth has been made a place of worship and purification for me. Whenever the time of prayer begins for any one of my Ummah (followers) he can pray wherever he is. The spoils of

---

16

war have been made lawful for me. I have been granted intercession. And every prophet was sent particularly to his own people, whereas I have been sent to all people".
(Bukhari & Muslim)

This does not suggest a lack of belief in earlier messengers or scriptures: Jesus perfected the religion of Moses, and Muhammad perfected the religion of Jesus, and Muhammad closed the chain of prophets and messengers; peace be upon them all. It is part of the complete faith of a Muslim to believe in all the revealed books and prophets before the Prophet Muhammad, and anyone who does believe in all, or any, of them, then he will be a non-Muslim. This is clear from the Prophet's statement when he was asked about belief. He (pbuh) said:

"It is to believe in Allah, His angels, His books, His messengers, the Hereafter and the divine Decree of good and evil." (Muslim)

6. Islam is distinguished for its divine laws and instructions, which are not man-made and so they are free from defects and faults and from the impact of surrounding effects such as culture, heritage and environment. This is evident in reality: human laws and legislation are alterable – what fits one community may not fit another. For example laws and regulations of a capitalist society do not go well with the conditions of a socialist one, and vice versa. Each legislator would choose what is in agreement with his aspirations and inclinations. In addition, such laws are unstable, for a more informed and knowledgeable person may object, rescind or add to the work of an earlier legislator.

Islamic law is however ordained by Allah. Its legislator is the Creator of the whole universe and all beings. He also knows all and is aware of all that is suitable for them and all that will bring them benefit in their affairs. Humans, however high their rank may be, have no right to object to or change any divine law, whether by increase or decrease or choosing what agrees with their desires and whims. Allah, glory to him said, (the meaning of which is translated as):

"And it becomes not a believing man or a believing woman, when Allah and His Messenger have decided an affair (for them), that they should (after that) have any claim in their affair." (The Qur'aan, Chapter Al-Ahzab, 33:36)

He also said, (the meaning of which is translated as):

"Is it a judgement to a people of the time of (pagan) ignorance that they are seeking? Who is better than Allah for judgement to a people who have certainty (in their belief)?." (The Qur'aan, Chapter Al-Mai'dah, 5:50)

Islam has introduced absolute, comprehensive and perfect rules and fundamentals that are not subject to change and revision with the elapse of time. It, nevertheless, left particulars and details that are not explicitly stated in the Qur'aan and Sunnah. Therefore, the responsible, authoritative and erudite scholars everywhere at any time may exert their effort to derive and infer verdicts and provisions that are in the public interest which suit the prevailing conditions in human societies at various times and environments. This religious reasoning and investigation – called Ijtihad – is not to be controlled by prejudices and desires but aims to reach truths that are of use to humankind, so that Islam should keep up with, and adapt its detailed regulations with every age and society. The role of the Muslim government is to bring those divine laws and rules into force and enforce them on everyone, without distinguishing between the rich, the poor, between the noble, the lowly, between the president, or the chief and his subjects, nor between the whites and the blacks. All people are alike and equal before the law.

Bukhari and Muslim narrated, on the authority of A'isha, may Allah be pleased with her, that the Quraysh tribes were concerned about the case of a Makhzumi woman who was accused of theft. They said: "Who will plead on her behalf with Allah's Messenger, peace be upon him?" Some of them suggested – "Who other than Usamah Ibn Zaid, whom the Prophet loves very much, can do so?" As such, Usamah represented her case to the Prophet, who told him:

"Do you intercede in the matter of a grave crime involving punishment prescribed by Allah? "

So saying, he got up and delivered an address in which he said:

"The people who preceded you were destroyed because they use to let noble person go if he committed theft, while punishing a weak person who committed the same crime. By

Allah, if Fatimah, daughter of Muhammad, had committed this offense I would have cut off her hand".

7. Islam is distinguished by the fact that its texts and sources are original, genuine and intact (with no addition or omission). They are of permanent, eternal authenticity and validity up till the Day of Resurrection. Basic sources of Islamic Shariah are the Qur'aan and the Noble Sunnah. Allah, Exalted be He, has undertaken to preserve the Qur'aan He said, (the meaning of which is translated as):

"Lo! We, even We, have revealed the Reminder (i.e. the Qur'aan) and Lo! We verily are its Guardian." (The Qur'aan, Chapter An-Nahl, 15:9)

Since its revelation onto Muhammad,(pbuh)up to the present, the Qur'aan had not undergone any change, distortion, increase or decrease. Many attempts have been made from the side of those who plotted against Islam to add or delete one word, but their efforts ended in failure. That is because it was preserved in books and memories as it was recited in prayer or as a form of worship. According to the Gracious Prophet (pbuh):

"Whoever recites one letter from the Qur'aan will get one good reward, and that reward will be equal in recompense to ten good deeds. I do not say that 'Alif Lam Meem' is a letter, but 'Alif' is a letter, 'Lam' is a letter and 'Meem' is a letter." (Tirmidhi)[4]

The Prophet (pbuh) also said:

"The best among you are those who have learned the Qur'aan and taught it (to others)." (Bukhari)

For these reasons the Muslims earnestly hastened to teach the Qur'aan to others.

Many a Western scholar admitted the excellence of the Qur'aan and its influence on human thought and sciences. Of such scholars there is

---

[4] This is in reference to the recited phrase "Alif-Lam-Meem" which appears at the beginning of a number of chapters of the Qur'aan, particularly nos. 2 and 3. Each phonetic word represents the initial of an Arabic letter, so as such it is not an actual word.

Margoliouth,[5] who was famous for his prejudices against Islam. Yet the greatness of the Qur'aan did not deter him from telling the truth when he pointed out that,

> *"Researchers are all agreed that the Qur'aan occupied an outstanding rank among the dignified religious scriptures that made history, though the latest of them in revelation. It has surpassed all in its marvelous impact on man. It has created a new human thought and established a unique moral school."*

According to Jean Melia:[6]

> *"It is a must to discard the pretension of some French philosophers. The Qur'aan should be recited slowly and deliberately. It has nothing of the charges of opponents that it preaches bigotry. Islam is a heavenly revealed religion, a religion of love, affection and honor, and the most tolerant of faiths."*

Hart Wighischfield[7] held that;

> *"One need not feel surprised if it is said that the Qur'aan is the source of sciences. All that the Qur'aan has talked about, such as the earth, human life, trade and craft, was the subject-matter of study by scholars and commentators who shed light thereon in their books and commentaries on the Qur'aan. This opened up a broad latitude of research and reflection which paved the way for the advancement of science by Muslims. Its influence was not limited to Arabs. It caused Jewish philosophers to follow in the steps of Arabs in metaphysical questions of religion. It is needless to mention the benefits that Christian theology has derived from Arab research in theology."*

Then there is the case of the Prophet's Sunnah, meaning his traditions, or acts, statements and confirmations. They are transmitted through a verifiable chain of transmitters, to the Prophet Muhammad (pbuh). As such the Sunnah represents the second source of the

---

[5] Margoliouth, Introduction to the Koran. Rev. J. M. Rodwell. London 1918.
[6] Jean Melia:Le Coran Pour La France.
[7] Hartwig Hirshfeld:New Researches into Composition and Exegesis of the Qur'aan. London 1902, p.9

Islamic Law and the exponent of the Qur'aan and its verdicts. The Sunnah has also been preserved from abuse, invention and interpolation, through reliable chains of transmitters known for their integrity and soundness of memory. Such transmitters were upright scholars who devoted their lives to the study of narration from Allah's Messenger.

Their chains of narration, texts, degree of authenticity, and status of their narrators and transmitters serve as a declaration of their eligibility or invalidation. As such, they sifted through all of the traditions (Hadiths) narrated from the Prophet and accepted only authentic ones, so they reached us pure and free from false narration. If one desires to know the way of Sunnah preservation, he can refer to books on the Hadith Science which was established to serve the Prophet's Hadiths, so that he may make sure about the certainty and authenticity of the Prophets' traditions we have received.

8. Islam considers all people equal in regard to their origin and birth, both male and female. Allah, glorious is He, first created Adam, the father of all humanity, and created from him, his wife Eve – the mother of humanity. He made them the origin of all human offspring. The Qur'aan declares human equality in their origin:

"O mankind! fear your Lord, Who created you from a single soul and from it created its mate, and from them both a multitude of men and women have spread abroad. Be careful of your duty toward Allah in Whom you claim (your rights) of one another and toward the wombs (that bore you)... " (The Qur'aan, Chapter An-Nisa'a, 4:1).

The Prophet Muhammad (pbuh) said:

"People are the children of Adam and Adam was (created) from dust." (Imam Ahmad).

All humans that exist or that ever will exist, are of Adam's progeny. They began with one religion and one language; but being large in number, they spread throughout the earth. This inevitably led to difference of color and nature. This included different ways of thinking and living and different beliefs. The Qur'aan states, (the meaning of which is translated as):

"Mankind was but one community, then they differed... " (The Qur'aan, Chapter Yunus, 10:19).

Islamic instructions place man, regardless of his race, color, tongue, religion and homeland, on equal terms with his brethren, all equal before Allah. However, differences and conflict arise among them in as much as they are close to, or far from, compliance with Allah's Law and way of life. The Qur'aan states, (the meaning of which is translated as):

"O mankind! Lo! We have created you from male and female, and have made you nations and tribes that you may know one another. Lo! The noblest of you in before Allah, is the most pious of you..." (The Qur'aan, Chapter Al-Hujarat, 49:13).

Based on this equality confirmed by Islam, all people are equal in freedom in the sight of Islamic Law. This slogan was launched by Caliph 'Umar Ibn Al-Khattab fourteen centuries ago when, criticizing someone's harshness, he said:

"When did you enslave people whose mothers bore them free?"

All should have access to:

- Freedom of thinking and opinion. The Prophet, (pbuh) required his companions to tell the truth and express their views fearing no blame when he, (pbuh) said:

"He who holds back from telling the truth is silent devil."

The Prophet's Companions, may Allah be pleased with them, put this principle into effect. One man addressed 'Umar Ibn Al-Khattab saying: *"Fear Allah, Commander of the Believers!"* One man protested saying: *"You say this to the Commander of the Believers!"* 'Umar said: *"Let him say it. You are useless if you do not say it, and we are useless if we do not accept it from you."*

On another occasion, when 'Umar was asked why he did not repute or reject Ali's judgement, as it was in conflict with 'Umar's, he answered: *"Had the matter been stated in the Qur'aan and Hadith I would have rejected it. But it is a matter of opinion and opinion is common and nobody is sure which of the two views is more right according to Allah."*

- Everyone is free to own property and earn his living as stated in the Qur'aan, (the meaning of which is translated as):

"...Unto men a portion from that which they have earned, and unto women a portion from that which they have earned..." (The Qur'aan, Chapter An-Nisa'a, 4:32)

- Everyone should be given the chance to be educated, as stated by the Prophet (pbuh),

"Seeking knowledge is every Muslim's duty." (Baihaqi).

Islam requires scholars to disseminate knowledge and not to hide it, so that everyone may benefit by it. This is stated by the Prophet (pbuh):

"Whoever is asked about some knowledge, yet he conceals it, he will be bridled on the Day of Judgement with a bridle of fire." (Abu Dawood and Tirmidhi).

- Everyone has the right to utilize the resources deposited in this universe by its Creator. The Qur'aan says, (the meaning of which is translated as):

"He it is Who made the earth subservient unto you, so walk in the path thereof and eat of His provisions. And unto Him will be the resurrection (of the dead)." (The Qur'aan, Chapter Al-Mulk, 67:15).

- Everyone may have given to leadership in society if he is worthy and capable of it. Prophet Muhammad (pbuh) said:

"If a person is placed in authority over Muslims and he appoints a man over them out of prejudice (in favor of him), Allah's curse be upon him, and Allah will not accept any good deeds from him, until He throws him into hell-fire." (Al-Hakim).

All this should be within the framework of Islam, and no aspect of freedom should be in conflict with the freedom of others. Philosopher and Historian, A. J. Toynbee, in his book, "Civilization on Trial", states,

"Putting an end to racial discrimination and tribalism has been one of the greatest feats and prides of Islam. It is in fact the biggest need of this age. Undoubtedly, English speaking

---

nations have achieved a certain degree of success in inter-linking of peoples and have given mankind good and mercy, but it should be admitted that they failed to get rid of racial and national sentiments."

9. Islam has no independent spiritual powers like those given to the clergy in other religions. That is because, when it came, it eliminated all intermediaries that are placed or installed between God (Allah) and His servants. It criticized idolaters for their adoption of intermediaries in worship, as appears from the Qur'aanic verse that relates their false argument, (the meaning of which is translated as):

"We worship them only that they may bring us near unto Allah." (The Qur'aan, Chapter Sad, 38:3).

Then Allah, Glory to Him, makes clear to them the true nature of these intermediaries, (the meaning of which is translated as):

"Lo! Those whom you call besides Allah are servants like you. So call on them now and let them answer you, if you are truthful." (The Qur'aan, Chapter Al-A'raf, 7:194).

Thus Islam has established and stabilized the concept of direct God-man relationship on the basis of absolute belief in Allah and His revealed ordinances and way of life. Forgiveness must be sought directly from Him with no intermediaries. Whoever commits a sin should raise his hands and pray humbly to Allah for forgiveness. This is clear from the following words , (the meaning of which is translated as):

"Whoever does evil or wrongs his own soul, then seeks pardon of Allah, will find Allah Forgiving, Merciful." (The Qur'aan, Chapter An-Nisa'a, 4:110)

Islam, unlike other religions, has no clergymen who permit and prohibit as if they were – and they actually consider themselves as– responsible on behalf of Allah for His servants. Consequently, they legislate for them, control their beliefs and admit whom they will into paradise and prevent whom they will. Allah, Glory to Him says about them, (the meaning of which is translated as):

"They have taken as lords besides Allah their rabbis and their monks..." (The Qur'aan, Chapter At-Tawbah, 9:31).

Prophet Muhammad (pbuh) explained:

"They did not worship them; only they obeyed them when they made something lawful or unlawful for them." *(Tirmidhi)*

10. Islam gave the individual rights that are due to them from society as well as rights due in the interest of all: The individual works in the interest of society and vice versa. The Prophet (pbuh) said: *"The bonds of brotherhood between two Muslims are like parts of a building, one part strengthens and holds the other."* Then he crossed the fingers of one hand between those of the other (to illustrate the point). (Bukhari)

However in case of conflict between individual and collective interests, the latter are to have priority over the former. As in the case of demolishing a house about to fall or taking out part of it to be added to the street in the public interest (of course after compensating the owner of the house). For example, a man from the Ansar (Muslims immigrants) had a fruit garden. In that garden there were a number of palm trees owned by a man called Samura Ibn Jundub, who used to go into the garden for his palm trees, but he caused harm to the garden and its owner. The owner complained about that to the Prophet (pbuh), so he said to Samura: *"Sell him the palm trees."* Samura refused. The Prophet, (pbuh) said: *"Pull them out."* He refused. Therefore, the Prophet, (pbuh) said to him: *"You are causing harm."* Then he addressed the garden owner saying: *"Go and pluck out his palm trees."*

11. Islam is the religion of mercy, pity and sympathy. It called to giving up severity and rudeness and following the Prophet's example as described in the Qur'aan, (the meaning of which is translated as):

"It was by the mercy of Allah that you were lenient with them (O Muhammad), for if you had been stern and fierce of heart they would have dispersed from about you..." *(The Qur'aan, Chapter Ali 'Imran, 3:159)*

The Prophet (pbuh) said in this connection:

"Merciful people are worthy of Allah's Mercy. Show mercy to those living on earth and you will receive mercy from the One Who is in Heaven (Allah)." *(Tirmidhi).*

25

Islam has established kind and merciful treatment for all people, even with enemies. This is clear in the Prophet's (pbuh) commandment, (the meaning of which is translated as):

"Treat prisoners of war kindly."

If this is the Prophet's direction about prisoners of war that fight against Muslims, what would you expect his directions would be about peaceful people?

Islam extended its mercy and sympathy even to animals, as seen from the following tradition:

"A woman was thrown into Hell-fire because she shut up a cat until it died. She neither gave it something to eat and drink nor let it pick up its food from the insects and other vermin of the earth." (Bukahri & Muslim).

The Prophet Muhammad, (pbuh) once saw a donkey which had been branded on its face, upon which he said:

"Allah's curse be on him who has branded it." (Muslim).

Ibn 'Umar, may Allah be pleased with him, once passed by some boys who had made a bird a target and were shooting arrows at it. Ibn 'Umar asked:

"Who has done this? May Allah's curse be upon the person who did this. Allah's Messenger, peace be upon him, has cursed the man who makes a living thing a target for shooting. (Bukhari & Muslim).

Once the Prophet (pbuh) passed by a camel whose belly was sticking to his back (due to hunger). On this he remarked:

"Fear Allah and observe your duty to Him with these inarticulate animals..." (Abu Dawood).

If such is Islam's mercy towards animals, how then would be its mercy towards man, whom Allah has honored more than all other creatures. Allah, glory to Him, says, (the meaning of which is translated as):

"Verily We have honored the children of Adam. We carry them on the land and the sea, and have made provision of good things for them, and have preferred them above many

of those whom We created with a marked preference." (The Qur'aan, Chapter Al-Isra', 17:70)

Islam has not only required mercy for animals; it has also made it a means of forgiveness from sins and a way to Paradise. This is clear from the following tradition:

"A very thirsty man walking along a path found a well and descended into it. He drank water to his fill and came out, then he saw a dog with its tongue licking up the mud to quench his thirst. The man said to himself that the dog was feeling the same extreme thirst as he had felt a little while before. So he descended once more into the well, filled his leather case with water and came up holding it by his teeth and gave the dog a drink. Allah appreciated this act of this man and forgave his sins." The Prophet, peace be upon him, was asked: "Messenger of Allah, are we rewarded for kindness towards animals as well?" He said: "There is recompense for kindness to every living thing." (Bukhari).

12. Islam is not a religion of monasticism, celibacy, sepration from worldly life and devote it for the sake of the Hereafter, and abstention from enjoyment of good things created by Allah for man. The Prophet (pbuh) said:

"Allah, glory to Him, is pleased to see the effect of His Favors on His servant." (Tirmidhi).

Islam is not a religion that allows uncontrolled indulgence in this worldly life; it is a religion of moderation that embraces both religious and secular affairs and considers them as complementary to each other; no one aspect should prevail at the expense of another. Allah, glorious is He, points this out, (the meaning of which is translated as):

"But seek, with that which Allah has bestowed on you, the abode of the Hereafter, and neglect not your portion of the world, and be kind even as Allah has been kind to you." (The Qur'aan, Chapter Al-Qasas, 28:77)

The Glorious Qur'aan has enjoined, in several verses, balancing the spirit and the body, so it instructed man to remember his physical needs pertaining to earning his living while being busy with worship, (the meaning of which is translated as):

*"And when the prayer is ended, then disperse in the land
and seek of Allah's bounty..." (The Qur'aan, Chapter Al-
Jumu'a, 62:10)*

It also called man, while preoccupied with worldly matters and
concerns, to remember his spiritual needs by performing the devotions
prescribed by Allah, He said, (the meaning of which is translated as):

*"Men whom neither merchandise nor sale beguiles from
remembrance of Allah and performance of prayer and
paying to the poor their due; who fear a day when hearts
and sight will be overturned."(The Qur'aan, An-Nur, 24:37)*

Islam has introduced a way of life that preserves the rights of spirit,
body and mind in accordance with a divine Law which keeps people
away from going to extremes. As a Muslim is required to control his
soul and bring it to account for its acts, Allah said, (the meaning of
which is translated as):

*"And whoever does good an atom's weight will see it then,
And whose does ill an atom's weight of evil will see it then."
(The Qur'aan, Az-Zalazlah, 99:7-8),*

The Prophet (pbuh) said,

*"A wise person is one who keeps a watch over himself and
calls it to account and does good deeds in preparation for
the Hereafter; whereas a helpless person is one who pursues
his desires blindly and yet expects from Allah the fulfillment
of his futile desires." (Imam Ahmad),*

Man is also required not to fail to enjoy the good things made lawful
for him by Allah, including food, drink, clothing and marriage, as
stated in the Noble Qur'aan , (the meaning of which is translated as):

*"Say: 'Who has forbidden the adornment of Allah which He
has brought forth for His servant and the good things of His
provisions?...'" (The Qur'aan, Chapter Al-A'raf, 7:32)*

Islam has forbidden only what is harmful for man, in his body,
wealth or society. The human soul has been created by Allah and
made viceroy in the earth so as to abide by His Law, Allah said, (the
meaning of which is translated as):

"He it is who has placed you as successer upon the earth and has exalted some of you in rank above others, that He may try you by (the test of) that which He has given you..." *(The Qur'aan, Al-An'am, 6:165)*

Allah has created for this soul, or spirit, a harmonious and integrated body. He says, (the meaning of which is translated as):

"Surely We created man of the best stature." (The Qur'aan, At-Tin, 95:4)

That is in order that the soul should perform, by means of the body; devotions, rights, duties, construction and population of the earth as enjoined by Allah. Therefore, Allah has ordered that the body should be maintained and cared for:

- By purification and cleanness, Allah said, (the meaning of which is translated as):

"...Truly Allah Loves those who turn unto Him in repentance, and loves those who purify themselves." (The Qur'aan, Al-Baqarah, 2:222)

He has required ablution (wudu') as a prerequisite to the integrity of prayer performed by Muslims five times a day the Prophet (pbuh) said,

"No prayer is valid without performing ablution (wudu')" (Abu Dawud).

It has also urged performing a ritual bath (ghusul) for Friday Prayer. The Prophet (pbuh) said,

"A bath (ghusul) on Friday is a duty recommended for every adult (Muslim), along with siwak (natural toothbrush) and whatever perfume possible." (Bukhari & Muslim).

Ritual bath is obligatory in case of major ritual impurity (janaba) Allah said, (the meaning of which is translated as):

"...And if you are unclean (after sexual discharge or intercourse), purify yourselves (i.e. bath your whole body)..." (The Qur'aan, Al-Mai'dah, 5:6)

- By cleanness; i.e. by cleaning both hands before and after meals, in compliance with the Hadith of the Prophet (pbuh),

"The blessing of food is (realized) by ablution prior to it and ablution following it." (Imam Ahmad).

And also by cleaning the mouth, as recommended by the Prophet (pbuh),

"It is recommended for one who has eaten to pick his teeth: whatever he picks he should expel from his mouth and whatever he chews he should swallow." (Ad-Darimi).

Also the Prophet (pbuh) said,

"Had I not feared that it would cause inconvenience to my people, then I would have ordered them to use siwak before every prayer." (Bukhari & Muslim).

As well as removing what can be a breeding ground for germs and dirt, in accordance with the Prophets' (pbuh) saying,

"There are five practices of pure nature: removal of hair from private parts, circumcision, removing hair from the armpits, trimming the moustache, and clipping of nails." (Bukhari & Muslim).

- By instructing man to eat and drink only lawful things, as evidenced by the Noble Qur'aan, (the meaning of which is translated as):

"O you who believe! Eat of the good things wherewith We have provided you, and render thanks to Allah if it is (indeed) He whom you worship." (The Qur'aan, Chapter Al-Baqarah, 2:172).

Such eating and drinking of lawful things are conditional upon avoidance of extravagance where the bad effects of which are quite evident, Allah said, (the meaning of which is translated as):

"... And eat and drink, but be not extravagant. Lo! He love not the extravagant." (The Qur'aan, Chapter Al-A'raf, 7:31)

Prophet Muhammad (pbuh) said,

"Man has never filled a pot worse than his stomach. However, if he insists on doing it, a third (of his stomach) should be apportioned to his food, a third to his drink and a third to his breath." (Imam Ahmad).

• By forbidding him to eat or drink what is bad or unlawful (such as carrion, blood, swine-flesh, wine, drugs and smoking) for securing the safety of the body. The Qur'aan says, (the meaning of which is translated as):

"He has forbidden you only carrion, and blood, and swine-flesh, and that which has been sacrificed to other than Allah. But he who is driven by necessity, neither craving nor transgressing, it is no sin for him. Lo! Allah is All-Forgiving, All-Merciful." (The Qur'aan, Chapter Al-Baqarah, 2:173)

• By encouraging the practice of sports, such as wrestling (without exposing private parts or hurting others), swimming, shooting, horseback riding and racing (foot racing). According to Ayesha, the Prophet's wife, may Allah be pleased with her:

"Allah's Messenger, peace be upon him, raced with me and I won. That was before I filled out. Later he raced with me when I was heavier and he won." He said: "This was for that." (Imam Ahmad)

"Allah's Messenger, peace be upon him, wrestled with Rukana and won." (Abu Dawud)

The Prophet, peace be upon him, also said:

"Teach your children shooting, swimming and horse-riding." (Muslim)

• By treatment of the body in case of sickness. According to the Prophet's (pbuh) saying,

"Take medicine, for Allah has never sent down a disease without sending down a cure for it, some people know it and others do not know it." (Imam Ahmad).

- By performing the prescribed devotions that provide the spirit with its nutrition and save it from anxiety which affects the body.

Islam doesn't prescribe neglect, torture or deprivation of the body. According to Anas Ibn Malik, may Allah be pleased with him; three men called at the houses of the Prophet's wives to ask about his devotions. When they were told about them they found it less than they expected. They said: *"What are we to compare with Allah's Messenger, peace be upon him, whose lapses, past and future are forgiven?"* One of them said: *"As for me, I shall spend my nights praying forever."* The second said: *"As for me, I shall fast daily forever and never break my fast".* The third said: *"As for me, I shall abstain from women and never marry".* Then the Prophet (pbuh) came to them and asked them, *"Is it you who said such and such? Listen, I swear in Allah, I am more pious and have more fear of Allah than you, yet I pray and sleep, fast and break (my fast), get married to women. Whoever deviates from my Sunnah (way or line of conduct) he is not of me."* (Bukhari & Muslim).

According to a Muslim German Scholar, Muhammad Asad;

"Islam does not regard the world, like Christianity, through black binoculars, yet it teaches us not to overestimate the worldly life, like the contemporary western civilization. Christianity scorns and condemns this worldly life, while the contemporary west – unlike the Christian spirit – is highly involved and deeply interested in this life. Islam, on the other hand, neither scorns nor overestimates it; it gives it due respect and consideration and at the same time deems it as a stage of our journey to a higher life – just a means and not an end. Islam guides us to pray: 'Our Lord! Give unto us in the world that which is good and in the hereafter that which is good.'[8]

13. Islam promotes knowledge and learning, and at the same time it disapproves of, and warns against ignorance. It classifies science into two categories:

a) Sciences whose learning is an individual duty prescribed upon every Muslim – both religious and worldly.

---

[8] Adapted from Mohammed Asad:Islam at the Cross-roads, Fifth Edition, P.29

b) Sciences whose learning is a collective duty prescribed upon an adequate number of people. The Qur'aan points out, (the meaning of which is translated as):

"...Are those who know equal with those who know not?..." *(The Qur'aan, Chapter Az-Zumar, 39:9)*

"... Allah will exalt those who believe among you, and those who have knowledge, to a high rank..." (The Qur'aan, Chapter Al-Mujadila, 58:11)

"...And say, 'My Lord! Increase me in knowledge.'" (The Qur'aan, Chapter Ta-Ha, 20:114)

The blessed Prophet, (pbuh) said,

"Seek knowledge even it were in China." He also says: "On the Day of Judgement, the ink of scholars will be weighed with martyr's blood."

Monsieur Casanova, one of the senior professors of College de France in Paris, commented on these traditions (Hadiths) saying:

"Many of us think that Muslims cannot assimilate our opinions or digest our concepts, forgetting that the Prophet of Islam is the one who stated that knowledge is superior to devotions. Who among the higher ranks of the clergy and priests has the courage to utter such decisive strong words, such words that are the essence of our contemporary intellectual life?"

Islam also respects scholars and gives them their due rank and rights. This is evident in the Prophet's (pbuh) words,

"A person who does not respect our elders, has no compassion for our children, and does not recognize the rights of our scholars is not from my people." (Imam Ahmad)

He (pbuh) said,

"The virtue of a scholar over a worshipper is like that of my virtue over an ordinary Muslim among you." (Tirmidhi)

Islam regards the search for knowledge and teaching an aspect of Jihad (i.e. strife in the cause of Allah) that is rewarded by Allah. This is stated in the following Hadith of the Prophet (pbuh),

"A person who goes out (of his house) in search of knowledge is on Allah's way and he remains so till he returns." (Tirmidhi)

He (pbuh) also said,

"If a person follows a path for acquiring knowledge, Allah will make the passage to Paradise easy for him." (Muslim)

Islam has not limited its exhortation of knowledge to religious sciences only. It has also encouraged secular sciences and considered learning them an aspect of worship that is rewarded by Allah (those considered as collective duty) as mankind is in need of such sciences or fields of knowledge. The Qur'aan says, (the meaning of which is translated as):

"So let man consider what he is created from. He is created from a gushing fluid, that issues from between the loins and ribs. (The Qur'aan, Chapter At-Tariq, 86:5-7)

The Qur'aan also says, (the meaning of which is translated as):

"Have you not seen that Allah causes water to fall from the sky and We produce therewith fruit of diverse hues, and among the hills are streaks white and red, of diverse hues, and (others) raven-black; And of men and beasts and cattle, in like manner, diverse hues? The erudite among His servants fear Allah alone. Lo! Allah is All-Mighty, Oft Forgiving." (The Qur'aan, Chapter Al-Fatir, 35:27-28)

These verses contain an invitation to sound thinking and meditation which leads to recognition of the existence of a Creator of these things and to benefiting from the resources and treasures of this universe. Certainly, the "erudite" in this verse are not only religious scholars; they are also erudite scholars and scientists in all fields of human knowledge who posses the ability to know the secrets and mysteries of this universe.

For example the process of cloud formation or rainfall can only be understood through familiarity with chemistry and physics. The growth of trees, plants and fruits through familiarity with agriculture; the variation in the colors of the earth and mountains through familiarity with geology; the nature and character of people, their different races and the nature and instincts of animals, through ethnology and zoology. Seldillot stated in his book, 'The History of Arabs',

"Muslims in the Middle Ages were unrivalled in science, philosophy and arts. They disseminated such knowledge whenever they moved, then it was carried over to Europe where it led to its renaissance and advancement."

Dr. G. Lebon, in his book, 'Arab Civilization', states that,

"We have never seen in history a nation so prominent in its impact as the Arabs, for all peoples that had relations with the Arabs embraced their culture even for a while."

14. Islam is the religion of self-control. It trains its adherents to seek Allah's pleasure in both their religious and worldly endeavors, as indicated in the Prophet's (pbuh) Hadith,

"Fear Allah, wherever you may be, do a virtuous act after an evil act as the former will undo the latter, and behave well with the people." (Tirmidhi).

The way adopted by Islam in rooting the principle of self-control and internal monitoring is as follows:

First: It has made Muslims believe in One God Who has no partner in Sovereignty or equal to Him, i.e. :Allah, Glory to Him. The Qur'aan declares, (the meaning of which is translated as):

"Say, He is Allah, the One; Allah, the Eternally Besought of All. He begets not, nor He is begotten; and there is none like unto Him." (The Qur'aan, Chapter Al-Ikhlas, 112:1-4)

• This God is the Originator and Creator of this world, along with all things in it, animate and inanimate. Allah said in the Qur'aan, (the meaning of which is translated as):

"Glory be to Him Who created all the pairs, of that which the earth grows, and of themselves, and of that which they know not!" (The Qur'aan, Chapter Ya-Sin, 36:36)

• This God is the Lord and Owner of all creatures; to Him belong sovereignty, commandment and the right to forbid, and He is ever able to do everything, Allah said, (the meaning of which is translated as):

"Lo! Your Lord is Allah Who created the heavens and the earth in six days, then He the ascended over the Throne (in the manner that suits His Majesty). He covers the night with the day, which is in haste to follow it, and has made the sun and the stars subservient by His command. His indeed is all creation and commandment. Blessed be Allah, the Lord of the Worlds!" (The Qur'aan, Chapter Al-A'raf, 7:54)

• This God possesses all attributes of perfection, Allah said, (the meaning of which is translated as):

"...There is nothing whatsoever like unto Him, and He is the All-Hearer, the All-Seer." (The Qur'aan, Chapter Ash-Shura, 42:11).

• He, glory to Him, knows well everything that is going on or taking place in this Universe at all times, He said, (the meaning of which is translated as):

"... He knows all that enters the earth and all that emerges therefrom and all that comes down from the sky and all that ascends therein; and He is with you where-so-ever you may be and Allah is All-seer of what you do." (The Qur'aan, Chapter Al-Hadid, 57:4)

Moreover, His knowledge goes beyond visible and tangible things to thoughts and emotions, He said, (the meaning of which is translated as):

"He knows the deceit of the eyes, and all that the breast conceals." (The Qur'aan, Chapter Al-Mu'min, 40:19)

Second: Islam has ingrained the concept of resurrection after death in Muslims and deemed it one of its basic principles, Allah said, (the meaning of which is translated as):

"Those who disbelieve assert that they will not be raised again. Say (unto them, O Muhammad): 'Yes verily, by my Lord! You will be raised again and then you will be informed

of what you did, and that is easy for Allah.'" (The Qur'aan, Chapter At-Tagabun, 64:7)

Third: Islam has established and rooted the idea that man is to be brought to account before Allah, glory to Him, for all his deeds and words whatsoever – large or small, good and bad, then recompensed according to his acts – good for good and evil for evil. Such feeling drives him to seek Allah's pleasure by complying with Allah's commands and avoiding His prohibitions, doing everything good and shunning anything bad, He said, (the meaning of which is translated as):

"And whoever does good an atom's weight will see it then, And who-so does an atom's weight of evil will see it then." (The Qur'aan, Chapter Az-Zalzalah, 99:7-8).

Fourth: Islam requires its followers to give precedence to obedience of Allah, seeking His pleasure and avoiding His prohibitions over everything and everybody else whosoever, even if this were in conflict with their desires, for the sake of winning Allah's reward in Paradise and escaping His punishment in Hell-fire. However, Islam has not ignored the physical aspects of punishment for those who rebel against its instructions and disobey its directives. Some people would require force to deter them from committing violations that are harmful to them and to their society. That is why Islam assigns for each crime a punishment that matches the extent of its seriousness. It has prescribed retaliation for intentional murder, Allah said, (the meaning of which is translated as):

"O you who believe! Retaliation is prescribed for you in the matter of the murdered..." (The Qur'aan, Chapter Al-Baqarah, 2:178)

This is the case if the heir of the murdered does not forgive them, Allah said, (the meaning of which is translated as):

"...And for him who is forgiven somewhat by his (injured) brother..." (The Qur'aan, Chapter Al-Baqarah, 2:178)

For robbery it has prescribed cutting off the hand, He said, (the meaning of which is translated as):

"As for the thief, both male and female, cut off their hands. It is the reward of their own deeds: an exemplary punishment

from Allah. Allah is All-Mighty, All-Wise." (The Qur'aan, Chapter Al-Ma'idah, 5:38)

When a thief is sure that his hand will be cut off if he steals, he will give up theft and thereby save his hand, and at the same time people's property and money will be safe from robbery.

Islam prescribes flogging in case of trespassing upon honor and modesty, i.e. in case of fornication, Allah said, (the meaning of which is translated as):

"The woman and the man guilty of fornication, scourge you each one of them (with) a hundred stripes..." (The Qur'aan Chapter An-Nur, 24:2)

For false accusation against chaste women (of adultery), it has prescribed eighty stripes, Allah said, (the meaning of which is translated as):

"And those who accuse honorable women (of adultery) but bring not four witnesses, scourge them (with) eighty stripes..." (The Qur'aan, Chapter An-Nur, 24:4)

The Islamic Law sets a general rule for penalties, Allah said, (the meaning of which is translated as):

"The recompense of a harm is a harm the like thereof..." (The Qur'aan, Chapter Ash-Shura, 42:40)

Allah said, (the meaning of which is translated as):

"If you punish, then punish with the like of that wherewith you were afflicted..." (The Qur'aan, Chapter An-Nahl, 16:126)

Islam has not made such penalties inevitable: it has left the way open to forgiveness, Allah said, (the meaning of which is translated as):

"...Let them forgive and show indulgence..." (The Qur'aan, Chapter An-Nur, 24:22)

"But whosoever pardons and amends, his wage is the affair of Allah..." (The Qur'aan, Chapter Ash-Shura, 42:40).

When it decides to implement these penalties, Islam does not aim at revenge and the spread of violence. It aims at preserving rights of people, establishing security and peace in society, and deterring those who intend to disturb its peace and stability. When a murderer realizes that he will be executed, a thief that his hand will be cut off, an adulterer that he will be flogged, they will be deterred from committing their crime and thereby maintain their own and other's safety and security. The Qur'aan sums up this truth, (the meaning of which is translated as):

"And there is life for you in retaliation, O men of understanding." (The Qur'aan Chapter Al-Baqarah, 2:179)

One may say that the penalties ordained by Islam for certain crimes are cruel! The response to this is that everyone agrees these crimes are evidently harmful to society and must be fought and retaliated against; conflict and disagreement only exists over the kind of punishment. Let everybody ask himself and decide: Are the penalties prescribed by Islam more viable and effective to root out or minimize crime, or man-made legislative punishments?

15. Islam points out that good acts are multiplied and that good intention is to be rewarded even if it is not followed by action, Allah said, (the meaning of which is translated as):

"Whoever brings a good deed will receive ten-fold the like thereof, while whoever brings an evil deed will be awarded but the like thereof." (The Qur'aan, Chapter An-An'am, 6:160)

The Prophet, (pbuh) said, (the meaning of which is translated as):

"Intention determines the worth of a person's actions and he will attain what he intends." (Bukhari & Muslim)

Moreover, if a Muslim intends to do a good deed for fear of Allah's wrath, he will be rewarded for that. The Gracious Prophet (pbuh) said,

"One who makes up his mind to do a good deed but does not carry it out, is rewarded by Allah for one full measure of it, and if he then proceeds to carry it out, Allah rewards him from ten to seven hundred times and even many times more. He who makes up his mind to do an evil deed, but does not carry it out, is rewarded by Allah for one full measure of

good deed. Should he carry it out, he is debited only by one evil deed." (Bukhari & Muslim)

In addition, habits and permissible things turn into rewardable devotions when associated with good intention. Food and drink, for example, when associated with the intention to maintain the body and preserve its strength for earning a living and performing the prescribed devotions, as well as providing for one's family, will be regarded an aspect of worship that deserves Allah's reward. The Noble Prophet (pbuh) said,

"...To cohabit with your wife is charity".

He was asked: *"Is it possible that one of us should satisfy his desire and yet he would be rewarded?"* He said:

"Yes. If he satisfied his urge through illicit means, would it not be sinful? Likewise, when he satisfies it lawfully it is deserving reward." (Muslim)

According to Islam, rewards are multiplied and the Muslim will be rewarded for a good intention, even if he does not implement it. Allah said, (the meaning of which is translated as):

"Whoever brings a good deed shall have ten times the like thereof to his credit" (The Qur'aan, Chapter Al-An'am 6:160)

16. According to Islam, sins are replaced with good deeds if sinners are sincere in their repentance and determined never to return to their sins. The Qur'aan states in this context, (the meaning of which is translated as):

"And those who do not invoke any other god along with Allah, nor take the life which Allah has forbidden save in (course of) justice, nor commit adultery – and whoever does this shall pay the penalty. The doom will be doubled for him on the Day of Resurrection, and he will abide therein disdained forever. Save him who repents and believes and does righteous work: as for such, Allah will change their evil deeds to good deeds, Allah is ever Forgiving, Most merciful" (The Qur'aan, Chapter Al-Furqan, 25:68-70)

This is for what is due to Allah. As for rights of people, they should have access to them and apology should be offered to them for any pain or suffering caused. Examples include beating, abuse, backbiting and slander; but in case of trespassing on people's property and the like, the trespasser will have to return what is due to the owner them to ask their forgiveness. Islamic Law has addressed the sinner's mind directly and treated his of her troubled mentality by opening the way to repentance so that he or she should be deterred from sin. Allah said, (the meaning of which is translated as):

> "Say: O my servants who have transgressed against themselves(by sinning), Despair not of the mercy of Allah, for verily Allah forgives all sins." (The Qur'aan, Chapter Az-Zumar, 39:53)

> "Yet whoever does evil or wrongs his own soul, then seeks pardon of Allah, will find Allah ever forgiving, All-Merciful." (The Qur'aan, Chapter An-Nisa'a, 4:110)

That is for Muslims. As for non-Muslims who embraced this religion, they will be given a double reward on account of their belief in their own messenger, besides their belief in the message of Muhammad, peace be upon him, The Qur'aan said, (the meaning of which is translated as):

> "Those unto whom We gave the Scripture before it, they believe in it. And when it is recited unto them, they Say: 'We believe in it. Lo! It is the truth from our Lord. Lo! Even before it we were of those who surrender (unto Him).' These will be given their reward twice over, because they are steadfast and repel evil with good, and spend of that wherewith We have provided them." (The Qur'aan, Chapter Al-Qasas, 28:52-54)

In addition, Allah will erase all their sins which they committed before accepting Islam, for the Gracious Prophet (pbuh) said,

> "Islam undoes all (ill-deeds) that has been done before (embracing) it."

17. Islam ensures for Muslims the continuation of good deeds even after death through virtuous endeavors and ongoing charitable acts, so long as they are beneficial to the whole society. The Gracious Prophet (pbuh) said,

"After the death of a person his actions stop, except three things that he leaves behind: 1) Continuous charity, (2) Knowledge from which some benefit may be obtained, and 3) a righteous child who prays for him." (Bukhari & Muslim)

He (pbuh) said,

"A person who invites others to righteousness shall have a recompense equal to the recompense of those who follow his guidance without reducing their recompense. A person who invites others to error shall have a share of punishment equal to that due to those who follow him without reducing their punishment." (Bukhari & Muslim)

18. Islam highly values the human mind and encourages sound reasoning. It liberates it from the fetters of heathenism and mental bondage. There is no need for anybody or anything to interfere or intercede with Allah on behalf of His creation – All are equal before Allah, Who addresses mankind, (the meaning of which is translated as):

"Lo! In the heavens and the earth are portents (signs) for the believers. And in your creation, and all the beasts that He scatters in the earth, are portents for a folk whose faith is sure: And the alternations of night and day and the provision that Allah sends down from the sky and thereby revives the earth after her death, and the ordering of the winds, are portents for a people who have sense." (The Qur'aan, Chapter Al-Jathiya, 45:3-5)

Islam criticizes those who imitate and follow older generations without knowledge or guidance, Allah said, (the meaning of which is translated as):

"And when it is said unto them: 'Follow that which Allah has revealed.' They say: 'We follow that wherein we found our fathers.' What! Even though their fathers understood nothing and had no guidance?" (The Qur'aan, Chapter Al-Baqarah, 2:170)

It is common in the Glorious Qur'aan to address the human mind: *"Have they then no sense?" "Will they not then ponder...?" "Will you not then take thought?"* Islam, however, has determined the domain of mental activity: The human mind should be used to perceive the visible and tangible; it has no access to the unseen which cannot be perceived by the senses, and engaging the mind with such things is a mere dissipation of efforts and energies.

19. Islam has liberated the human soul from being blindly controlled by others, imbuing it with conviction that none other than Allah can quicken the dead or cause death or harm. So no man, whatever his race, color, or position is, can benefit or harm, deprive or give, unless Allah, Glory be to Him, wills so. The Qur'aan states, (the meaning of which is translated as):

> *"...And (they) possess not hurt nor profit for themselves, and possess not death nor life, nor power to raise the dead."*
> *(The Qur'aan, Chapter Al-Furqan, 25:3)*

If Allah's Messenger, peace be upon him, despite his high rank with Allah, is subject to what applies to other people: What would be the case for others? The Qur'aan says, (the meaning of which is translated as):

> *"Say: 'For myself I have no power to benefit, nor power to hurt, save that which Allah wills. Had I knowledge of the Unseen, I should have abundance of wealth, and adversity would not touch me. I am but a warner, and a bearer of good tidings unto folk who believe." The Qur'aan, Chapter Al-A'raf, 7:188)*

It has also freed the human mind from anxiety, fear and confusion, by treating their causes:

- If the cause is fear of death, it is stated in the Noble Qur'aan, (the meaning of which is translated as):

> *"No soul can ever die except by Allah's Leave and at a term appointed..."(The Qur'aan, Chapter Al-'Imran, 3:145)*

However hard man tries to escape death, it is lying in wait for him. The Qur'aan says, (the meaning of which is translated as):

> *"Say: 'Lo! The death from which you flee will surely meet you..." (The Qur'aan, Chapter Al-Jumu'a, 62:8)*

- If it is fear of poverty, it is made clear in the Qur'aan, (the meaning of which is translated as):

"...There is not a beast in the earth but the sustenance thereof depends on Allah. He knows its habitation and its place. All is in a clear record." (The Qur'aan, Chapter Hud, 11:6)

- If it is fear of disease and misfortunes, Allah said, (the meaning of which is translated as):

"If Allah touches you with affliction, there is none that can relieve it save Him, and if He desires good for you, there is none who can repel His bounty. He strikes with it whom He wills of His servants..." (The Qur'aan, Chapter Yunus, 10:107)

The Qur'aan also states, (the meaning of which is translated as):

"No disaster occurs in the earth or in yourselves but it is in a Book before We bring it into being – Lo! That is easy for Allah. That you grieve not for the sake of that which has escaped you, nor yet exult because of that which has been given to you. Allah does not love any prideful boaster." (The Qur'aan, Chapter Al-Hadid, 57:22-23)

20. Islam does not order tasks that are beyond the scope of human ability. It is the religion of facility, simplicity, moderation, reasonableness, and freedom from hardship. This is stated in the Glorious Qur'aan said, (the meaning of which is translated as):

"Allah tasks not a soul beyond its scope. For it (is only) that which it has earned, and against it (only) that which it has deserved..."(The Qur'aan, Chapter Al-Baqarah, 2:286)

The Prophet, (pbuh) said:

"Allah has not sent me as a self-opinionated (messenger) nor to make others self-opinionated; but as a teacher and to facilitate things for people." (Muslim)

He, (pbuh) said:

"Make things easy and convenient and don't make them harsh and difficult. Give cheers and glad tidings and do not create hatred." (Bukhari).

He, (pbuh) said:

"If I order you to do something, do what you can thereof." *(Bukhari).*

Once a man came to Allah's Messenger (pbuh) and said, *"O Allah's Messenger! I have been ruined."* Allah's Messenger, (pbuh) asked: *'What was the matter with you'.* He replied, *"I had sexual intercourse with my wife while I was observing fast."* Allah's Messenger, (pbuh) asked him: *"Can you afford to free a slave?'* He replied in the negative. Allah's Messenger (pbuh) asked him: *"Can you observe fast for two successive months?"* He replied in the negative. The Prophet (pbuh) asked him: *"Can you afford to feed sixty poor people?"* He replied in the negative. The Prophet kept silent and while we were in that state, a big basket full of dates was brought to the Prophet, (pbuh) He asked: *"Where is the questioner?"* He replied, *"I (am here)."* The Prophet (pbuh) said to him: *"Take this (basket of dates) and give it in charity."* The man said, *"Should I give it to a person poorer than I? By Allah; there is no family between it's (Al-Madinah's) two mountains poorer than mine."* The Prophet smiled till his molar teeth became visible and then He (pbuh) said: *"Feed your family with it."* (Al-Bukhari)

All principles and devotions of Islam are in harmony with human abilities, they do not tend to overburden them, so that people may have no excuse for neglecting such principles and devotions, taking into consideration that they can be dropped in cases of necessity. For example:

- One of the obligatory acts of prayer is standing if able. In case of the inability to stand, a worshipper may perform the prayer in a sitting posture; if not then in a reclining posture; if not then by gesturing. Likewise, Congregational Prayer at a Mosque is obligatory for men, but such an obligation is dropped in case of sickness, fear, extreme cold or heavy rain. Another example is relieving a woman in her menstrual cycle or post-natal period of prayer until ritual impurity is over; she is not required to make up for the missed prayer.

- Payment of Zakat (the poor-due) is not required of those who do not possess the minimum amount of money, property or assets set for the imposition of Zakat.

- A person who is too sick or too old to fast is exempt from fasting. A traveler and a woman in her menstrual cycle or post-natal period, are exempt from fasting until such conditions have ended. They merely make up for the days they have not fasted later.

- Those who are physically or financially incapable of Hajj during its season are exempt from its duty, until they are capable. In which case the physically incapable person will have to delegate someone to perform Hajj on his behalf. The Qur'aan states, (the meaning of which is translated as):

"... And pilgrimage (Hajj) to the House is a duty unto Allah for mankind, for him who can bear the journey..." (The Qur'aan, Chapter Ali 'Imran,3:97)

- If a person is afraid he will die, he is allowed to keep himself alive with unlawful food or drink, such as carrion, blood, pork or wine, provided he finds nothing lawful to eat or drink. The Qur'aan says, (the meaning of which is translated as):

"...But he who is driven by necessity, neither craving nor transgressing, it is no sin for him..." (The Qur'aan, Chapter Al-Baqarah, 2:173)

In his commentary on this verse, Sayyed Qutb said:

"It is the creed which acknowledges man as human, not as an animal, angel or devil. It recognizes him with all his weaknesses and strengths, takes him as one entity comprising a body with its desires, a mind with its power of reasoning and a spirit with its hopes and aspirations. It also prescribes for him obligations that he can afford and observes balancing and coordination between obligations and ability without causing any hardship or overburdening him".

21. Islam urges people to abstain from slander and to respect others' feelings by refraining from insulting their religious beliefs. In the Qur'aan, it is stated, (the meaning of which is translated as):

"Revile not those unto whom they pray besides Allah, lest they wrongfully revile Allah through ignorance..." *(The Qur'aan, Chapter Al-An'am, 6:108)*

22. Islam encourages meaningful dialogue which guides to the Divine Path and good manners, Allah said, (the meaning of which is translated as):

"Say: O People of the Scripture! Come to a word agreed upon between us and you, that we worship none but Allah, and that we associate no partners with Him, and that none of us shall take others for Lords besides Allah. Then, if they turn away, Say: "Bear witness that we are Muslims." (The Qur'aan, Chapter Ali 'Imran, 3:64)

23. Islam is the religion of middle-of-the-road and moderation in matters of both religion and worldly life. The Qur'aan states said, (the meaning of which is translated as):

"Thus We have made you a medium nation (Ummah), that you may be witnesses over mankind, and that the Messenger may be a witness over you..." (The Qur'aan, Chapter Al-Baqarah, 2:143)

Thus Islam is:

- Middle-of-the-road as regards prophets between those who held extreme views about them (like Christians) and those who were harsh to them (like Jews), since Muslims believe in all prophets and behave towards them with all due respect and love.

- Moderate in all Sharia – related matters: Islam is free from the strictness and burdens of the Jews and from the extreme indulgence and negligence of the Christians.

24. Islam considers every good deed performed by a Muslim an act of charity, as pointed out by the Prophet, (pbuh):

"Charity is necessary for every Muslim."

He was asked: *"What if a person has nothing?"* The Prophet replied;

"He should work with his own hands for his benefit and also give (something out of such earnings in) charity".

The companions said: *"And if he is not be able to work?"* The Prophet (pbuh) said:

"He should help the poor and needy people."

They said: *"And if he cannot do even that?"* The Prophet said,

"He should urge others to do good".

The companions said: *"And if he doesn't do that also?"* The Prophet said:

"Let him stop himself from doing evil: That is charity also (for him)". (Bukhari)

The Prophet, (pbuh) said:

"Do not consider even the smallest good deed as insignificant; even meeting your bother with a cheerful face (is a good deed)." (Muslim)

25. Islam orders Muslims to preserve the environment and refrain from causing any environmental pollution whatsoever:

- By urging them to plant useful trees, the Prophet (pbuh) said:

"If a Muslim plants a tree, then whatever is eaten from it be human or animals is a charity." (Muslim)

- By urging them to remove all that is harmful, the Prophet (pbuh) said:

"Removing anything which causes harm from the path of others is charity." (Bukhari & Muslim)

- By urging them to apply voluntary quarantine, as this is called for in the Prophet's (pbuh) words:

"If you hear of plague in a land, then do not go there, and if it occurs in a land (you are in) then do not run away from it." (Bukhari & Muslim).

This is just to prevent epidemics and infectious diseases from being passed on to others and to save the lives of people.

- By warning them against killing birds, animals or other creatures without reasonable cause or purpose. The Prophet (pbuh) said:

"Whoever kills a bird in vain, that bird says to Allah Almighty on the Day of Judgement: 'O Lord! So-and-so killed me just for fun and not for any good purpose.'" (Imam Ahmad and Nasa'i)

- By warning them against contaminating public utilities such as water sources, in view of the Prophet's Hadith in this regard related on the authority of Jabir, may Allah be pleased with him, that Allah's Messenger (pbuh) prohibited urinating in standing water. (Muslim)

- And, finally, by warning them against any acts that cause environmental damage on earth. Allah, Glory to Him, says, (the meaning of which is translated as):

"Work not corruption in the earth after its reformation, and call on Him in fear and hope. Lo! The mercy of Allah is (ever) near unto the good-doers." (The Qur'aan, Chapter Al-A'raf, 7:56)

He also says, (the meaning of which is translated as):

"And when he turns away (from you) his effort in the land is to make mischief therein and to destroy the crops and the cattle; and Allah loves not mischief. And when it is said unto him: Be careful of your duty to Allah, pride takes him to sin. So Hell will be enough for him (as punishment), an evil resting-place." (The Qur'aan, Chapter Al-Baqarah, 2:205-206)

26. Islam is the religion of all-embracing peace, in the full meaning of the word. Both on the internal level of the Muslim society: (as pointed out by the Prophet, (pbuh))

"The (true) Muslim is one from whose tongue and hand all Muslims are safe, and (true) emigrant is one who leaves those things which Allah has prohibited." (Bukhari & Muslim) Also: "A (true) believer is from whom people are secure."

And on the global level on basis of establishing friendly relations that are based on security, stability and non-aggression between the Muslim society and other societies, especially those societies that do not play with religion, as stated in the Qur'aan, (the meaning of which is translated as):

"O you who believe! Come all of you, into submission (Islam) unto Him: and follow not the footsteps of Satan. Lo! He is an open enemy for you." (The Qur'aan, Chapter Al-Baqarah, 2:208)

In order to maintain such peace, Islam instructs Muslims to repel attacks and fight against oppression. This is stated in the Qur'aan, (the meaning of which is translated as):

"... And one who assaults you, assault him in like manner as he assaulted you..." (The Qur'aan, Chapter Al-Baqarah, 2:194)

To demonstrate its interest in peace and antipathy against oppression, murder and terrorism, Islam orders its adherents, even in case of war, to accept peace and stop fighting when the enemy requests that, Allah said, (the meaning of which is translated as):

"But if they incline to peace, you also incline to it, and (put your) trust in Allah. Verily, He is the All-Hearer, the All-Knower." (The Qur'aan, Chapter Al-Anfal, 8:61)

While Islam is keen on peace, it does not mean that its adherents should be humiliated for the sake of peace. Rather, it instructs them to maintain peace while keeping their pride and dignity intact. The Qur'aan states, (the meaning of which is translated as):

"So be not weak and ask not for peace (from the enemies of Islam) while you are having the upper hand. Allah is with you and He will never decrease the reward of your good deeds." (The Qur'aan, Chapter Muhammad, 47:35)

27. Islam makes it a rule that embracing it should emanate from full conviction devoid of coercion. In the Noble Qur'aan it is stated, (the meaning of which is translated as):

"There is no compulsion in religion. Verily, the Right Path has become distinct from the wrong path." (The Qur'aan, Chapter Al-Baqarah, 2:256)

And:

"And Say: 'The Truth is from your Lord.' Then whosoever wills, let him believe; and whosoever wills, let him disbelieve..." (The Qur'aan, Chapter Al-Kahf, 18:29)

It is part of Islam's tolerance and justice to give people the freedom to choose their belief. It holds that mankind is free to accept or reject its teachings and that Jews or Christians who refuse to embrace it are completely free to practice their beliefs and doctrines without undergoing any kind of oppression or harassment that affects such practice. It is never allowed to ruin their churches or break their crosses, for the Prophet (pbuh) said:

"Leave them to practice their own religion."

Islam also gives them the freedom to have the foods or drinks deemed lawful by their religion, so their pigs should never be killed and their wine should not be spilt. As for civil affairs, such as marriage and divorce cases and financial transactions, they have the full freedom to behave according to their beliefs.

'Umar Ibn Al-Khattab, may Allah be pleased with him, put this into action. While he was once inside a church in Jerusalem, the call to prayer was announced, upon which he went out of the church for prayer and said to the Patriarch: *"I'm afraid if I prayed within the church that Muslims after me would say this is the praying place of 'Umar and then demolish it and build a Mosque in its place.."* (Tabari).

According to the famous historian, Tabari, 'Umar granted them a guarantee of security for themselves, their property, churches and crosses: that no damage or destruction shall be allowed to be inflicted on them, nor shall any coercion or oppression be practiced against them in matters of religion.

28. Islam is the first religion to call to the liberation of creatures, while prohibiting many forms of slavery: It closed all the doors to human bondage, except for one, i.e. through captivity from war, subject to conditions. This is clear from the fact that Islam narrowed the sources of slavery and expanded the outlets for emancipation, such as slave liberation in expiation of certain sins like:

- Killing by mistake. (as stated in the Qur'aan), (the meaning of which is translated as):

"He who has killed a believer by mistake must set free a believing slave, and pay the blood-money to the family of the slain, unless they remit it as a charity. If he (the victim) be of a people hostile unto you, and he is a believer, then (the penance is) to set free a believing slave. And if he comes of a folk between whom and you there is a covenant, then the blood-money must be paid unto his folk and (also) a believing slave must be set free..." (The Qur'aan, Chapter An-Nisa'a, 4:92)

- The violation of one's oath, Allah said, (the meaning of which is translated as):

"Allah will not take you to task for that which is unintentional in your oaths, but He will take you to task for the oaths which you swear in earnest. The expiation thereof is to feed ten of the needy with the average of that wherewith you feed your own folk, or the clothing of them, or the liberation of a slave..." (The Qur'aan, Chapter Al-Ma'idah, 5:89)

- Zihar,(Abstaining from one's wife by declaring that she is the same as one's mother and thereby not lawful for sexual relations) Allah said, (the meaning of which is translated as):

"Those who pronounce thihar among you (by saying their wives that they are as their mothers) and afterwards would go back on that which they have said, (the penalty) in that case (is) the freeing of a slave before they touch one another..." (The Qur'aan, Chapter Al-Mujadila, 58:3)

- Performing sexual intercourse while fasting in Ramadan.

- Setting slaves free, which was highly encouraged by Islam, with promises of great reward for the emancipator, Allah said, (the meaning of which is translated as):

"Did We not assign unto him two eyes, and a tongue and two lips, and show him the two ways (of good and evil)? Why has he not attempted the ascent? Ah, what will convey unto you

what the ascent is ! - It is to free a slave." (The Qur'aan, Chapter Al-Balad, 90:8-13)

The Prophet, (pbuh) said, (the meaning of which is translated as):

"A person who frees a Muslim slave, Allah will deliver everyone of his limbs from the fire of Hell in return for each of the limbs of the slave." (Bukhari & Muslim)

Writing of emancipation, (i.e. Mukatabah), which is an agreement between a master and his slave for emancipating the latter for an agreed amount of money. Certain jurists (especially Imam Ahmad, Allah's mercy be upon him) held that in case a slave requests a writing of emancipation it will be incumbent upon his master to respond positively, as stated in the Qur'aan, (the meaning of which is translated as):

"...And such of your slaves seek a writing (of emancipation), write it for them if you are aware of any good in them, and bestow upon them from the wealth of Allah which has bestowed upon you..." (The Qur'aan, Chapter An-Nur, 24:33)

Furthermore, Islam has made slave and captive emancipation one of the outlets for spending Zakat revenues or payment of one's Zakat (poor-due). The Qur'aan states, (the meaning of which is translated as):

"The alms (i.e.:Zakat) are only for the poor and the needy, and those who collect them, and those whose hearts are to be reconciled and to free the captives and the debtors, and for the cause of Allah, and (for) the wayfarers; a duty imposed by Allah. Allah is All-Knower, All-Wise." (The Qur'aan, Chapter At-Tauba, 9:60)

29. Islam encompasses all aspects of life – ideological, political, social, economic and moral. The Qur'aan says, (the meaning of which is translated as):

"...And We have sent down to you the Book (the Qur'aan) as an exposition of everything, a guidance, a mercy, and glad tidings for those who have submitted themselves (to Allah as Muslims)." (The Qur'aan, Chapter Al-Nahl, 16:89)

Allah's Messenger, (pbuh) said:

"Faith consists of seventy some branches, the highest of which is the testimony that there is no god but Allah, and the lowest is removing something harmful from the road. Modesty is one of the branches of faith." (Bukhari)

An evidence of such comprehensiveness is Islam's interest in human conduct and those particulars related to people's life. For example, Allah's Messenger, (pbuh) explains etiquette when entering or going out of the toilet, by saying:

"If one of you goes into the toilet, he should advance his left foot first and Say: 'In the name of Allah. O Allah ! I seek refuge in You from vicious males and female devils.' When he goes out, he should put his right foot first and Say: 'Praise be to Allah, Who has relieved me of nuisance and made me well.'" (Bukhari).

The Spiritual Side of Islam

Devotions (Form of Worship)

Islam contains a host of verbal, practical and ideological devotions. Verbal and practical devotions represent what are called the 'Pillars of Islam', and represent the basis on which we describe someone as Muslim or non-Muslim. Of these Pillars the two testimonies of faith are verbal, praying and fasting are physical, Zakat is financial and Hajj (Pilgrimage) is both physical and financial. Islam does not intend these pillars to be mere appearances: it aims at purifying and refining their souls through the performance of these devotions. It wants the performance of these pillars to be a means of reforming the individual. About prayer, the Qur'aan says, (the meaning of which is translated as):

"...The prayer prevents from great sins and evil deeds..."
(The Qur'aan, Chapter Al-Ankabut, 29:45)

About Zakat:

"Take alms from their wealth in order to purify them and sanctify them with it..." (The Qur'aan, Chapter At-Tauba, 9:103)

It purifies the soul of the filth of miserliness and avarice. About fasting:

"O you who believe! Fasting is prescribed for you as it was prescribed for those before you, that you may become righteous." (The Qur'aan, Chapter Al-Baqarah, 2:183)

It trains a person to refrain from indulgence in desires. This is explained by the Prophet's Hadith (pbuh) about fasting:

"If a person does not give up telling falsehood and acting according to it, Allah does not need his abstinence from eating and drinking." (Bukhari)

About Hajj:

"The Hajj is (in) the well-known months. So whosoever intends to perform Hajj, then he should not have sexual relations, nor commit sin, nor dispute unjustly during the Hajj..." (The Qur'aan, Chapter Al-Baqarah, 2:197)

Devotions then play an essential role in the establishment and enhancement of good morals.

The Pillars of Islam

1. The Two Testimonies of Faith

It is to testify that 'there is no god (worthy of worship) but Allah, and that Muhammad is the servant and Messenger of Allah.'

This verbal fundamental is the key to embracing Islam, and all other pillars of Islam are based on it. 'There is no god but Allah' means to deny the existence of any god worthy to be worshipped other than Allah, glory be to Him. To Him all kinds of devotions must be addressed, including supplication, wishes, hopes, sacrifice, bowing prostration, trust, vows, etc. He glory be to Him, is the Creator of everything that exists. He is also the Provider and the Absolute Sovereign. Allah said, (the meaning of which is translated as):

" And We sent no messenger before you but we inspired him, (saying: There is no God except Me (Allah), So worship me." The Qur'aan, Chapter Al-Anbiya', 21:25)

The testimony that 'Muhammad is Allah's Messenger' reflects the belief that he is the servant and messenger of Allah who received and conveyed divine revelation, that he was sent by Allah to all mankind as the final prophet. There will be no prophet or messenger is to come after him. He must be believed in and obeyed as he is the conveyor of Allah's message and guidance.

2. Observing Regular Prayer

The Islamic Prayer (salat) comprises words (including invocations and glorification of Allah) and acts (including prostration and bowing) performed in glorification and reverence for Allah. It gives man an opportunity to humbly commune with his Lord. It is, in fact, a link between Allah and His servant. Whenever man gets immersed in worldly pleasures and the light of faith begins to fade in his heart, the call to prayer is announced and the light in his heart is revived, keeping him near to, and on good terms with his Creator at all times.

Prayer is to be performed five times a day. Adult Muslim males perform these prayers in congregation in Mosques unless there is some excuse. Congregational prayer helps people to get acquainted with one another, it strengthens the bonds of friendship and affection between them and motivates them to look after each other: visiting the